ST. THOMAS AND
THE PROBLEM OF EVIL

The Aquinas Lecture, 1942

SAINT THOMAS
AND THE
PROBLEM OF EVIL

Under the Auspices of the Aristotelian Society
of Marquette University

BY

JACQUES MARITAIN

MARQUETTE UNIVERSITY PRESS
MILWAUKEE
1942

Nihil Obstat

Gerard Smith, S.J., censor deputatus
Milwaukiae, Die 13, Iunii, 1942

Imprimatur

Milwaukiae, Die 17 Iunii, 1942
Moyses E. Kiley
Archiepiscopus Milwaukiensis

PRINTED AT THE MARQUETTE UNIVERSITY PRESS
MILWAUKEE, WISCONSIN

THE AQUINAS LECTURES

The Aristotelian Society of Marquette University each year invites a scholar to speak on the philosophy of St. Thomas Aquinas. These lectures have come to be called the Aquinas Lectures and are customarily delivered on the Sunday nearest March 7, the feast day of the Society's patron saint.

This year the Society has the pleasure of recording the lecture of Prof. Jacques Maritain, lecturer in philosophy during alternate semesters at Columbia University and Princeton University.

Prof. Maritain was born in Paris on Nov. 18, 1882. He received his early education at the Lycée Henri IV, and his university education at the Sorbonne. He holds the doctorate in philosophy from the Sorbonne, as well as the agrégé de l'université. Following his schooling at Paris, he spent two years (1907-1908) in the study of biology at the University of Heidelberg. He has been professor of philosophy at the Institut Catholique de Paris since 1914, and at the Institute of Mediaeval Studies in the University of Toronto since 1933. In 1941 he was acting professor of philosophy at the University of Chicago. In January, 1942, he was the recipient of the Annual Christian Culture Award of Assumption College, Windsor, Ont. He is a frequent contributor to *The Commonweal* and to *Le Glaive de l'Esprit*, of which he is vice president.

An autobiographical essay by Prof. Maritain appeared in *I Believe* (1939), pp. 195-210. His biography has been written by his wife, Raissa Maritain, in her *Les grandes amitiés* (1941), which appeared in English translation under the title of *We Have Been Friends Together* (1942). An estimate of his philosophy is given in Gerald B. Phelan, *Jacques Maritain* (1937). A bibliography is to be found in Malachy Sullivan, "Jacques Maritain, Christian Humanist," *The Catholic Library World*, XIII (1942), 259-266, 291.

Among Prof. Maritain's very extensive writings are the following books with the titles of the English translations:

La philosophie bergsonienne (1914, 1930).

Art et scolastique (1920), *The Philosophy of Art* (1923), *Art and Scholasticism* (1927).

Introduction générale à la philosophie (1920), *An Introduction to Philosophy* (1930).

Théonas (1921), *Theonas, Conversations of a Sage* (1933).

Réflexions sur l'intelligence (1923).

L'ordre des concepts: I Petite logique (1923), *An Introduction to Logic* (1937).

Trois réformateurs (1925), *Three Reformers* (1928).

Primauté du spirituel (1927), *The Things That Are Not Caesars* (1930).

Le docteur angélique (1930), *The Angelic Doctor* (1931).

Religion et culture (1931), *Religion and Culture* (1931).

Le songe de Descartes (1932).

Distinguer pour unir ou les degrés du savoir (1932), *The Degrees of Knowledge* (1937).

De la philosophie chrétienne (1933).

Du régime temporel et de la liberté (1933), *Freedom in the Modern World* (1936).

Sept leçons sur l'être (1934), *An Introduction to Metaphysics* (1939).

La philosophie de la nature (1935).

Frontières de la poésie (1935).

Science et sagesse (1935), *Science and Wisdom* (1940).

Lettre sur l'indépendance (1935).

Humanisme integral (1936), *True Humanism* (1938).

Les juifs parmi les nations (1938).

Questions de conscience (1938).

Quatre essais sur l'esprit dans sa condition charnelle (1939).

Le crépuscule de la civilization (1939).

A Christian Looks at the Jewish Question (1939).

De la justice politique (1940).

Scholasticism and Politics (1940).

A travers le désastre (1941), *France, My Country Through the Disaster* (1941).

Ransoming the Time (1941).

La pensée de Saint Paul (1941), *The Living Thoughts of Saint Paul* (1941).

Confession de foi (1941).

To these the Aristotelian Society takes great pleasure in adding *Saint Thomas and the Problem of Evil*.

St. Thomas and the Problem of Evil *

I HAVE no intention of reviewing in one lecture all that St. Thomas has to say about the problem of evil. I should prefer,—keeping in mind the main characteristics of thomistic teaching concerning evil,—I should prefer to emphasize two points which I consider especially important: first, the meaning of the existence of evil in this world; second, the cause of evil where free will is concerned.

With regard to the metaphysics of evil, St. Thomas appropriates and develops the great themes made classical by St. Augustine: evil is neither an essence nor a nature nor a form nor an act of being—evil is an absence of being; it is not a mere negation, but a *privation*: the privation of the good that should be in a thing.[1]

That does not mean that evil does not exist, or is merely an illusion, or that we need only deny its existence, as do the Christian Scien-

---

* Translated by Mrs. Gordon Andison.

tists, to make it disappear. Evil does exist in things,[2] it is terribly present in them. Evil is real, it actually exists like a wound or mutilation of the being; evil is there in all reality, whenever a thing—which, insofar as it is, and has being, is good,—is deprived of some being or of some good it should have. Thus evil exists *in good,* that is, the bearer of evil is good, insofar as it is being.[3] And evil works *through good,* since evil, being in itself a privation or non-being, has no causality of its own.[4] Evil is therefore efficacious not by itself but through the good it wounds and preys upon as a parasite, efficacious through a good that is wanting or is deflected, and whose action is to that extent vitiated. What is thus the power of evil? It is the very power of the good that evil wounds and preys upon. The more powerful this good is, the more powerful evil will be,—not by virtue of itself, but by virtue of this good. That is why no evil is more powerful than that of the fallen angel. If evil appears so powerful in the world of today, that is because the good it preys upon is the very spirit of man,—science itself and moral ideals corrupted by bad will.

That that which has no being in itself, nor essence nor form, nor order, nor determination, and cannot have,—in other words, that evil exists, is real and efficacious,—it is in this that appears to us evil's metaphysical monstrosity. The whole spectacle of things is that of a procession of things good, of a procession of goods, wounded by non-being and producing by their activity an indefinitely-increasing accumulation of being and of good, in which that same activity also carries the indefinitely-growing wound—as long as the world exists—of non-being and of evil.

Another point of doctrine in which St. Thomas faithfully takes up again the great tradition of Plato and St. Augustine, is that the evil which is a fault, and which affects man's will and his liberty, making him evil himself and offending the Principle of his being, is a greater evil than the one which consists in suffering, and which merely affects nature in us, without causing us to swerve from the line of our ultimate destiny, which is supratemporal, and without being opposed, as St. Thomas puts it, "to Good increate, to the Good of God Himself, to the fulfillment of the divine will and divine love by which divine good is loved for itself, and not only as it is participated in by the creature."[5] It is better to be punished than to be guilty.

II

I come now to my first point: what, according to St. Thomas Aquinas, is the meaning of the existence of evil in the world?

St. Thomas deals with the question in the *Summa Theologica, Prima Pars,* question 48, article 2: "Perfection of the universe," he tells us, "demands that there be some inequality in things, so that all degrees of being and of goodness may be filled. Now there is a degree of goodness whose attribute is that whatever is situated in that degree is good to such an extent that it can never fall from good. And there is another degree of goodness whose characteristic is that whatever is situated in that degree is good in such a way that it can fall from good."

Actually, you know, the first degree of goodness, strictly speaking, is reserved for God alone and for those blessed spirits who enjoy supernaturally the beatific vision. The second degree of goodness characterises the whole of nature; even the angels, who cannot sin in respect to natural order considered alone, are fallible in respect to the supernatural order; (and it follows from this that, in respect to the natural order as bound to the supernatural order and backed up by it, they are fallible in the natural order as well.)

"Perfection of the universe," St. Thomas continues, "requires therefore that there be some beings who can fall from goodness; and if there are beings who can fall from goodness, the result will be that such defection will in fact sometimes occur in those beings." For if it is in the nature of things that an event can happen, this event actually will happen sometimes. "Now, to fall from good, there is the actual evil. That is why evil is found in things: as well as the existence in them of the process of destruction or corruption, for corruption itself is a certain evil."

In the answer to the third objection, St. Thomas explains "that God, and nature, and all active good, does what is best with regard to the whole, but not what is best for each part taken separately, unless it is taken in relation to the whole. Now the whole itself which is the universality of created beings, is better and more perfect if there are in it certain things which can be lacking in good, and which consequently sometimes do lack good, God not preventing it. On the one hand this is due to the fact that it is not right for Providence to destroy natures, but to preserve them, as Dionysius says in chapter IV of *Names Divine;* and it is the very nature of things that the beings who can be lacking in good are so lacking from time to time; on the other hand, it is because, as St. Augustine says, *(Enchir.* cap. XI) the power of God is so great that even from evil can He extract good. And thus there would be much good lost if God permitted no evil to exist; fire would not be generated if [according to the Physics of old] air were not corrupted, and the life of the lion would not be preserved were not the ass put to death; and there would be no occasion to wonder at God's Justice or the patience of those suffering persecution, did the iniquity of persecutors not exist."—That is why St. Ignatius prayed that his Company should be persecuted to the end of the world:—which presupposes persecutors to accomplish it.

Well—were one to misread such a text one could confuse the position of St. Thomas with that of Leibnitz,—although they are diametrically opposed to one another. In the optimism of Leibnitz we are bound to see a rationalistic deterioration of Christian truths: the author of the *Theodicy* justifies God as Job's friends did, and the Scriptures warn us that God holds such advocates in horror.

A philosopher like Leibnitz adopts the truths contained in the text from St. Thomas I have just read, in a merely philosophical sense, and as a satisfactory answer given by pure philosophy; this philosopher, then, will tell us it is a good thing for a mother to bewail the death of her child, because the machine of the world required it in order to be more perfect. *Rachel plorans filios suos, et noluit con-*

solari . . . (Rachel bewailing the death of her sons and refusing to be consoled). Explain this Leibnitzian position to the mother in question, tell her this thing was necessary in order that every degree of being should be filled, and she will answer that she cares not one whit for the machine of the world,—let them give her back her child! And she will be absolutely right; for such questions are not resolved by the machine of the world but in the darkness of faith, and by the cross of Jesus.

St. Thomas knew—and certainly much better than we do—what I have just said, but he is a difficult author to understand; he hides himself in the light and never expresses his whole thought all at once: to understand his ideas on evil it is necessary not only to consult what he says in that particular question of the *Summa* where he considers things from the viewpoint alone of the metaphysics of nature, but also to examine the whole treatise on grace and the one on the redeeming Incarnation, and all the theological context of thomist doctrine.

In the text we just read St. Thomas considers reality from a particular point of view, from the point of view of the order of nature, of the universe as a *work of art* made by God, as a work of creative art (*hic mundus,* "this world," the Gospel says). But there is another point of view,—that of the moral and spiritual relations of created persons to one another and with God, which relates to the universe of *freedom* and presupposes the world of nature, but is quite distinct from it.

And it is because of this distinction that St. Thomas teaches that the free act as such, being not of this world, is beyond the grasp of the natural knowledge of the angels, (to which, however, is due everything *of this world* considered as God's work of art; for the free act is not a part *of this world,* but of an original universe of its own, the universe of freedom).

As for the universe of nature then, or the universe as a work of creative art we must say —according to the conception, rather pessimistic indeed but serenely so, which St. Thomas gives of nature—we must say that man and angel are parts of the created universe, and as parts of this universe it is normal, it is in the order of things that they be fallible; it is in the order of things that man be involved in sorrow, suffering and death, because by his very essence he is involved in nature which is corporeal, subjected to the change of production and destruction.

But at the same time,—and here we have the other aspect of the matter,—man and angel are both *persons,* and in that light not parts but real *wholes;* for the person signifies in itself, wholeness. Neither man nor even the angel are persons in the perfect and absolute state, but they are in a real sense persons,—however wretchedly that condition of person is realised in man.

And from this point of view the existence of evil in things injects into being an incongruity from which nothing can console us. *Et noluit consolari.* (And she refused to be consoled.) The sin of a man is the sin of a person, the disaster of a universe and a wounding of God (not as far as God's being is concerned but as concerns His love). The suffering of a man is the suffering of a person, of a whole. Here he is considered no longer as part of the universe, but insofar as he is a person he is considered as a whole, a universe to himself; to suffer that pain as part of the universe in the perspective of nature or of the world taken as God's work of art, does not do away with the fact that as far as the person is concerned it is an utter anomaly.

The person asks,—from a desire which is "conditional" and "inefficacious," but real and natural—to see the first cause in its essence, it asks to be *free without being able to sin,* it asks that it should not suffer, should not die. In the state of pure nature, these aspirations of the person would have remained forever unsatisfied; grace causes us to reach up toward a final state where these aspirations will be superabundantly satisfied by a gift which surpasses all nature, being a formal participation in the Deity.

We see there the most profound reason of suitability for the elevation of the intelligent creature to the supernatural order; I say reason based on fitness! Not on necessity, nor on justice. God could, without the least injustice, have created man in a state of pure nature, man would have been defrauded of nothing which his *nature* as such demands; but in actual fact God has created man in a state of grace; let us say that in actual fact he would not have created nature if He had not destined it for grace,—and this word carries us very far. Very far from Leibnitz. Any good belonging to the order of grace, St. Thomas says, is greater than all the good nature is capable of.

St. Thomas also teaches that the motive of the Incarnation is Redemption; it is to redeem sinful man. But why, in the doctrine of St. Thomas, did God permit the sin of Adam, if not for Christ, for the Incarnation and for redemptive grace? And then one could say that just as the sin of Adam was permitted for the sake of the redeeming Incarnation, so freedom that can err was created for the love of charity between God and creature.

Here you have the sort of considerations which make up the contexts in which we must place the texts I was reading a moment ago. In the perspectives I have just mentioned, which are those of theology or of a moral philosophy which is not merely philosophical but backed up by faith and theology, it seems to me that we can obtain a slightly better understanding of the problem of evil, which in truth is not a problem but a mystery. I do not say, moreover, that he who is at this moment a prey to evil can find satisfaction in any answer no matter how true it may be. The experience of that which is in itself without any consolation, the experience of death can be surmounted or, rather, absorbed only by another experience, of a divine order,—by the experience of paschal love. Yet it seems to me that we shall not be speaking exactly like the friends of Job if we say this. In the first place, the creature as such cannot be free unless it be free in a freedom that is kindred to nothingness, (because it is the freedom of a creature drawn from nothingness),—in a freedom, therefore, which as to the natural order, may be subject to failure; this surely must be clear, —a free creature, naturally impeccable, would be a squared circle. We find this expounded in a fundamental article of the treatise on angels (*Summa Theologica,* I, q. 63, a. 1). St. Thomas explains, "if one considers it in its nature,— abstraction made of gifts of grace fructifying in life eternal,—every intelligent creature thus considered is liable to failure. And if it happens that a creature—Christ, for example (as a man), or the Blessed—cannot fail or sin, it derives that quality necessarily from the gift of grace and not from the condition of nature;

for failing or sinning is deviating from the rectitude that the act accomplished should have, but that act alone is incapable of deviating from its rule, whose rule is the energy itself, the very operative virtue of the agent. If the hand of the craftsman were the very rule by which he cut wood, he could never cut the wood crookedly. Now the only, absolutely the only will that is the rule of its own operation, is the divine will; consequently it alone is impeccable, not liable to failure, and the will of any creature whatsoever, regarded in the light of what nature as such is capable of doing, involves by itself the possibility of failing or sinning." God, therefore, cannot make any creature who is naturally impeccable, any more than He can make a squared circle; these are not necessities independent of God which are forced upon Him from without as though God were subject to the Styx and to the Fates; —as Descartes reproached St. Thomas for disposing of the matter; these necessities themselves depend on His very essence as His intelligence sees it, seeing at the same time all those ways in which that very essence can be participated in. To annihilate these necessities one would have to annihilate first the very essence of God, and thus we must admit that God can no more create a being by nature impeccable, than He can cease to exist and to be what He is. It is the same sort of necessity,—one springs from the other.

That much being established, we can continue. If there are in the universe creatures free and intelligent, therefore fallible, it is doubtless because, from the point of view of nature as a work of divine art, the perfection of the universe as a whole composed of diverse parts, required that every degree in the scale of being should be filled.

But if such a universe has been created, having in its bosom intelligent creatures, free and subject to failure, let us not forget that the end of its creation lies in the universe of grace. As we stated a moment ago, God, in actual fact, would not have made nature if He had not destined it to grace.

Sin therefore, taken as a disaster of that whole which we call the person, and as an offense against God,—sin and the suffering and sorrow which form its retinue are not permitted for the greater perfection of the machine of the world, but for the consummation of a work of love which transcends the whole order of the world; they are themselves connected to the manifestation of divine goodness as transcending the very universe of creation and expressing itself in the universe of grace or of the transfiguration of love of created persons become God through participation.

The creature's liability to sin is thus the price paid for the outpouring of creative Goodness, which in order to *give itself personally* to the extent that it transforms into itself something other than itself, must be *freely loved with friendship's love and communion,* and which to be freely loved with friendship's love and communion must create *free* creatures, and which in order to create them free must create them *fallibly* free. Without fallible freedom there can be no created freedom; without created freedom there can be no love in mutual friendship between God and creature; without love in mutual friendship between God and creature, there can be no supernatural transformation of the creature into God, no entering of the creature into the joy of his Lord. Sin,—evil,—is the price of glory.

III

I pass on now to the second point I mentioned at the beginning of my lecture: the cause of evil in the case where the evil in question is the evil of free will,—evil, not only ontological or metaphysical, but moral.

We have here a particular case of *evil of action*. St. Thomas distinguishes, as you know, between the evil that wounds the action or operation of beings,—*evil of action*,—and evil which wounds the being itself of the agent,—*evil of being*. And he teaches in a very general way that evil of action or operation always arises from a certain presupposed defect in the being or the operative powers of the agent.[6]

Consider the case of the world of material nature, the case of natural agents, animate or inanimate bodies, each of which tends in virtue of the constitution of its nature toward a certain action or specific operation. When the action or the operation in question is bad or defective, the cause of that evil—*evil of action*

—is the agent itself insofar as it is deprived of a certain good or perfection that it should have, insofar as there is in its being or in its operative powers a defect, an evil—that is evil of being. Stuttering has as its cause the organs and nerve centers of speech insofar as they suffer from a weakness or an imperfection. In the world of nature, *evil of action* always presupposes another evil—*evil of being*.

As for evil of being itself, or ontological wounds, defects, distresses, pains and destructions suffered by beings at work in nature, this evil has its origin in these beings themselves, each of which is good, but whose characteristic action, also good, cannot be accomplished without accidentally going beyond the finality proper to the being in question, thus producing by accident some privation in another being. The action of each of the beings involved in matter is good in itself, but these beings cannot act without at the same time wounding one another. It is good that fire burns, but fire cannot burn without consuming something.

The action by which that living thing called a microbe nourishes itself and reproduces is a thing good in itself, but if the microbe in living its life attacks the tissues of the nerve centers of a human being, it will be the cause—by accident, by going beyond its own finality,—of the weakness or defectiveness, of the *evil of being* whence a disorder in the muscular movements (evil of action) arises in that human being. In the world of material nature, evil of being results from the opposition, from the opposing dynamism existing between natures, the good that is proper to the one and to which alone it tends of itself being thus linked to privation or evil undergone by another in actual fact.

But now let us consider the world of freedom, the world of free acts. In that case, what is the cause of evil of action? What, in the order of metaphysical connections, is it that causes free action to be bad, or, if I may be allowed to express it this way, bitten by nothingness? This is a particularly difficult problem. I believe St. Thomas is the only thinker who has considered it in all its difficulty, and I think the solution he proposes is one of the most original of his philosophical discoveries.

The general principle I mentioned a while ago remains the same: evil of action or of operation always derives from a certain presupposed defect in the being or the active powers of the agent, that is to say, in this case, in the will. But this time the defect itself, that failure in the being which is the root of evil of action, must be a *voluntary and free* defect, since it is the evil of a free action or a free choice which results from it. And furthermore, contrary to what happens in the world of nature, this defect itself must *not be an evil* or a privation, for if it were *an evil of the will in the very nature or in the physical being of the latter* we should not be dealing with a voluntary and free defect: the cause of this defect must be the will itself, not nature; but on the other hand if this defect were *an evil of the will in its free activity,* then the defect itself would already be an evil-free action, and we should be explaining the evil of free action by evil of free action, which would be a vicious circle.

What then is this defect,—what is that failure in being which is the metaphysical root of evil of action and which is itself free without, however, being already an *evil?*

Let us read what St. Thomas himself says on the subject in the *Quaestiones Disputatae, de Malo*. Here one must, he explains,[7] *"preconsider a certain defect in the will, a certain deficiency prior to the act of choice which is itself deficient*. And that is explained in the following manner: in all things wherever one factor exists as the rule and measure of the other, good in the one that is ruled and measured originates from the fact that it is ruled in conformity with the rule and measure,—the evil arises from its not being ruled or measured according to the rule." (We know it is thus in everything that is ruled by another rule than itself; it is only in God that the hand that acts is itself the rule.) "Suppose we take a craftsman who must cut wood in a straight line according to a certain ruler: if he does not cut it in a straight line, that is, if he makes a bad cutting, that bad cutting will be caused by the fact that the craftsman did not hold the ruler in his hand. Similarly, delectation and everything that happens in human affairs should be measured and ruled according to the rule of reason and of divine law. That the will *does not use* [let us take careful note of the simple negation expressed there]—that the will *does not make use of* the rule of reason and of divine law," that it does not have the ruler in its hand,—this then, is the absence or the deficiency "which must be considered in the will before the faulty choice in which alone moral evil consists. And for that very absence or that lack which consists in not making use of the rule," not taking the rule in hand, *"there is no need to seek a cause, for the very freedom of will, whereby it can act or not act, is enough."* The lack or defect which we are discussing has as its primary cause freedom itself, which can act or not act and which does not act, does not pay attention to the rule; and this defect comes, I do not mean in time but in ontological order, before the act of choice. Here we are at the very beginning; impossible to go any further back: a free defect, a defect of which freedom itself is the negative and deficient primary cause;—and it is the will thus in default which, acting with this defect, is the cause—*in quantum deficiens*—of moral evil.

But this defect that is a prior condition of evil and which depends on freedom, is not itself an evil. "This very lack," St. Thomas continues, "which consists in not paying attention in act to the rule, this lack considered in itself *is not an evil,* neither in the sense of an evil deriving from fault nor of an evil consisting of fault." There is as yet no fault or evil in the mere absence which consists in not actually considering the rule, "because the soul is not obliged, nor for that matter is it able, constantly to take the rule into consideration, in act."

What is required of the soul is not that it should always look to the rule or have the ruler constantly in hand, but that it should *produce its act* while looking at the rule. Now in the metaphysical moment we are examining here there is as yet no act produced, there is merely an absence of consideration of the rule, and it is only in the act which will be produced, in terms of that absence, that evil will exist. Therein lies an extremely subtle point of doctrine, one of capital importance. Before the moral act, before the *bonum debitum,* the *due good* which makes up the quality of this act and whose absence is a privation and an evil, there is a metaphysical condition of the moral act, which, taken in itself, is not a due good, and the absence of which consequently will be neither a privation nor an evil but a pure and simple *negation* (absence of a good that is *not* due), and that metaphysical condition is a *free* condition.

"That which formally constitutes the fault or moral evil," writes St. Thomas, "comes into being in this,—that *without* the concurrent consideration of the rule, the will *proceeds to the act of choice*. Thus the craftsman does not err in not always having his ruler in hand but in proceeding to cut the wood without his ruler. The faultiness of will does not consist in not paying attention in act to the rule of reason or of divine law, but in this:— that without taking heed of the rule it proceeds to the act of choice." Its fault lies in the fact that without considering the rule,—an *absence* of attention of which freedom alone is the cause,—*it proceeds to the act of choice,* which is consequently *deprived* of the rectitude it should have. "That is why St. Augustine says that the will is the cause of sin insofar as it is deficient and he compares that deficiency to silence, or to darkness, because it is a question of a deficiency which is a pure and simple negation," and not a privation. Here we are at the very core of the metaphysics of the evil of free will.

In the same article of the *Quaestiones Disputatae, de Malo,* the answer to the third objection, St. Thomas says again: "The failure preconsidered in the will before the sin is neither an evil consisting of fault nor an evil deriving from fault, but a mere negation." But not to consider the rule becomes a fault from the single fact that with this negation the will applies itself to the act. *"Accipit rationem culpae ex hoc ipso quod cum tali negatione se applicat ad opus."*

As you see, St. Thomas breaks up so to speak into two moments not chronological but ontological, the movement of the will in the evil act of choice. In the *first* moment there is an absence of consideration of the rule: and that, by virtue of the pure initiative of the created will as a defective primary cause,—I do not mean by the *action* of created will, since at that moment there is still nothing positive, there is as yet no action—I mean by the defective (and free) *initiative* of the created will. Considered in itself that moment does not yet constitute the fault, for it is a mere absence of a good (and not a due good). And in the *second* moment there is action produced with that absence, action which should have been ruled and which is not ruled, from the fact that there is not concurrent consideration of the rule. At the first moment the will has introduced an absence—the non-consideration of the rule,—and at the second moment the act it accomplishes issues forth in conformity with that absence, that is to say not in conformity with the rule, not ruled. Therefore there is sin. But the non-consideration of the rule is not yet the sin.

"For it is through the very application to action, *ex ipsa applicatione ad opus,* that the good this action is lacking in becomes *due,* that is, the good of considering in act the rule of reason and of divine law."

St. Thomas insists essentially upon that doctrine, but except in the text I have just read he recalls it so briefly[8] that one might run the risk of neglecting its importance and its pro-

fundity. Evil lies in acting without reference to
the rule; and in this concrete whole, acting
without consideration of the rule, there are
two moments to be distinguished, not with
regard to time but according to ontological
order: *first moment, not considering the rule,*
which is a negation, an absence, the lack of a
good which is not yet due; and *second moment, acting with that negation,* which, from
the sole fact that one acts with it, becomes a
privation, an absence of a due good in the
action.

Well then, the first moment, and this is
what is so extremely important especially for
the problems touching upon the connection
between uncreated freedom and created freedom,—the first moment is voluntary, it is free,
and it is not yet sin but the root of sin; it is a
certain nothingness, the nothingness of the
consideration of the rule, it is a certain nothingness introduced by the creature at the start
of his action; it is a mere absence, a mere nothingness, but it is the root proper of evil action.

We say then that it is a mere absence and we say in the same breath that man has need of himself *alone* to propound that negation, to introduce that nothingness,—as St. Thomas says: *ad hoc sufficit ipsa libertas voluntatis.* As concerns this lack, the very freedom of will is enough. It is a sort of nothing, it is a mere absence, an *absence of act* of which created freedom has the initiative: therefore we must join in our minds these two notions, to *have the initiative* not of an act, but *of an absence,* of a negation, of the non-consideration in act of the rule. This requires a particularly difficult mental effort, for the words we use can mean everything—even things that do not exist—only *ad instar entis,* (after the pattern of being) and because we have as a result a great deal of difficulty in conceiving of a free initiative which is not an action, but an initiative *to not act,*[9] to not consider the rule, the initiative of an absence.

This moment of non-consideration of the rule is so to speak the spiritual element of sin.

There is a moment of nature, not of time, where the creature has as yet done nothing, where it has as yet made no choice, (that is why there is as yet no fault, but mere negation or absence of being) and where nevertheless it has already done nothingness in the sense that it has not considered its rule, freely and voluntarily,—it has put an absence at the head of its acting, it has introduced the condition which will cause the texture of being to give way; that is why there will be faultiness now that it acts with that voluntary non-consideration; such an act will bear in itself the teeth-marks of nothingness.

Were we to put that into picturesque present-day language, we should say, in trying to express this initiative of non-being, this initiative of absence on which I have placed so much emphasis,—we should say that the will *nihilates,* that it *noughts;* it has an initiative, yet we can only translate that initiative by words which express action. But, it is an initiative of non-action: we must therefore necessarily have recourse to a paradoxical language and say that created will then "does nothingness," "makes non-being;" and this is all it can do by itself: not the act bitten into by nothingness,—for as far as it is action and being, it must also have the help of God,—but nothingness which bites into the act. It "makes" non-being, that is to say that in all freedom it undoes, or it non-does, or it noughts; the creature slinks, not by an action but by a free non-action or dis-action,—from the influx of the First Cause,—which influx is loaded with being and goodness—it slinks from it insofar as this influx reaches the free region as such, it renders this influx sterile, it *nihilates* it. It is there, in that region proper to freedom, that is manifest in the sharpest way, because in a free manner, the particular condition of the creature which St. Thomas pointed to when he said that what comes from nothingness tends by its nature toward nothingness.[10] That is the metaphysical grandeur of the universe of freedom: there, and only there can the creature do some-

thing by itsef alone, but that something consists in non-being, and that "doing" is an absence of action. All that it does by itself alone
is nothingness; namely, the actual non-consideration of the rule, through its free initiative,
—the non-consideration of that rule without
which the act it is about to do cannot be good.
It seems to me that that explains for us St.
Thomas' very significant phrase[11] that "the
first cause of our failure to receive grace comes
from us,—*defectus gratiae prima causa est ex
nobis.*" There then is something wherein the
creature is the first, the primary cause; there
then, is a line in which the creature is the first
cause, but it is the line of nothingness, and of
evil.

Here we have traced evil to its innermost
hiding-place; here the creature is the primary
cause, but negatively; I think we might sum-
marize that doctrine in the words of the Gospel: "Without Me you can do nothing." That
text can be read in two ways, and these two
interpretations clarify the whole problem of

created freedom in the face of divine freedom. "Without Me you can do nothing," means: Without Me you can not commit the slightest act in which there is being or goodness,—so much for the line of good; but if it concerns the line of evil, then the text should be otherwise interpreted, doing violence to the grammar: *"sine Me potestis facere nihil,"* without Me you can do nothingness, without Me you can introduce into action and being the nothingness which wounds them and which constitutes evil. St. Hildegarde complained that that very thing, that *nihil,* that nothing, could be done without God, she complained to God because without Him we could do nothingness, for she well knew that if we could do it only with Him, then we should never be able to do it, for with God only good and only being can be done. Quite obviously non-being can be "done" only without God.

If I have dwelt at great length upon the thomistic doctrine of non-consideration of the rule as the cause of evil in free action, it is because that doctrine seems to me to allow us to catch a glimpse of how the *first initiative* of evil—permitted by God to the extent that divine motion or grace is merely "sufficient" or *breakable*—comes from the creature alone, from his voluntary and free failure. It is another way of saying that God, as St. Thomas affirms, is in absolutely no wise the cause of moral evil.

In the case of good it is not the same. In the case of good the creature has doubtless the initiative of its good act, without which it would not be a free cause; but it has not the *first initiative*. It is God Who has the first initiative of the good act. And when the creature does not produce nothingness under grace (this is no merit in its part, for not to take the initiative of nothingness is not to do something, it is only not to move under divine action),—when the creature does not take the initiative of nothingness, then divine motion or grace merely sufficient or breakable fructifies of itself into *unbreakable* divine motion or into grace efficacious by itself.

Thus we must reason in two different ways according to whether we are considering the line of evil or the line of good. Such a dissymmetry is absolutely necessary from the very fact that the line of good is the line of being, and the line of evil is the line of non-being and of privation. God is the cause of all the being and goodness there is in things; He is not the cause of the evil in free will. Man does not render efficacious grace efficacious, but he can render sufficient grace sterile or undeveloped into efficacious grace. By himself alone he cannot merit, but by himself alone he can demerit.

In closing I should like to indicate that these considerations help us the better to understand that the divine scheme is not a scenario written at a previous time, which is later to be performed by creatures. The divine scheme is simultaneous, just as eternity itself, with every moment of time. And thus the will and the permission of God eternally determine this eternal plan with regard to the presence or absence, at each moment of time, of a moment of non-consideration of the rule in human free will, which in this way does or does not by its own deficient first initiative, fail divine action.

The French socialist, Georges Sorel, who was a friend of Charles Péguy, and whose books were carefully read by Mussolini and by Lenin, and who was very fond of theology, said one day that the crucial work of the philosophers, in the new age into which we are entering, would consist in recasting and penetrating more deeply into the problem of evil. As a matter of fact, we are surely called upon to build up a theory of evil if we are to interpret philosophically our time. I would suggest that the great philosophers to come, of whom Georges Sorel spoke, will find in Thomas Aquinas the basic principles for such a metaphysical construction.

NOTES

1. *Summa Theologica*, I, q. 48, a. 1. (Cf. *de Malo*, 1, 1; *Contra Gentiles*, III, cap. 7, 8 and 9; *Compend. theologiae*, cap. 115).

2. *Summa Theologica*, I, q. 48, a. 2, and ad 2.

3. *Ibid.*, I, q. 48, a. 3.

4. *Ibid.*, I, q. 49, a. 1.

5. *Ibid.*, I, q. 48, a. 6.

6. *Ibid.*, I, q. 49, a. 1. (Cf. *de Malo*, 1, 3; *Contra Gentiles*, II, cap. 46; III, cap. 10 and 13).

7. *De Malo*, 1, 3.

8. Cf. *Summa Theologica*, I, q. 49, a. 1, ad 3: "Dicendum quod malum habet causam deficientem aliter in rebus voluntariis, et naturalibus. Agens enim naturale producit effectum suum talem quale ipsum est, nisi impediatur ab aliquo extrinseco; et hoc ipsum est quidem defectus eius. Unde nunquam sequitur malum in effectu, nisi praeexistat aliquod aliud malum in agente vel materia, sicut dictum est. Sed in rebus voluntariis defectus actionis a voluntate actu deficiente procedit, inquantum non subiicit se actu suae regulae. Qui tamen defectus non est culpa, sed eum sequitur culpa ex hoc quod cum tali defectu operatur."

Summa Theologica, I-II, q. 75, a. 1, ad 3: "Dicendum quod, sicut dictum est, voluntas sine adhi-

bitione regulae rationis vel legis divinae, est causa
peccati. Hoc autem quod est non adhibere regulam
rationis vel legis divinae, secundum se non habet
rationem mali, nec poenae, nec culpae, antequam
applicetur ad actum."

Contra Gentiles III, cap. 10: "Relinquitur igitur
quod morale vitium in solo actu voluntatis primo et
principaliter invenitur; et rationabiliter, quum ex
hoc actus moralis dicatur quia voluntarius est. In
actu igitur voluntatis quaerenda est radix et origo
peccati moralis.

"Videtur autem hanc inquisitionem consequi
difficultas. Quum enim actus deficiens proveniat
propter defectum activi principii, oportet praein-
telligere defectum in voluntate ante peccatum
morale. Qui quidem defectus, si sit naturalis, semper inhaeret voluntati; semper igitur voluntas in
agendo moraliter peccabit, quod actus virtutum
falsum esse ostendunt. Si autem defectus sit voluntarius, jam est peccatum morale, cujus causa iterum
inquirenda restabit; et sic ratio in infinitum dedu-
cet. Oportet ergo dicere quod defectus in voluntate praeexistens non sit naturalis, ne sequatur
voluntatem in quolibet actu peccare; neque etiam
casualis, et fortuitus; non enim esset in nobis
morale peccatum; casualia enim sunt impraemedi-
tata et extra rationem. Est igitur voluntarius, non
tamen peccatum morale, ne cogamus in infinitum
procedere.

"Quod quidem qualiter esse possit consideran-
dum est. Cujuslibet siquidem activi principii per-

fectio virtutis ex superiori activo dependet; agens enim secundum agit per virtutem primi agentis. Quum igitur secundum agens manet sub ordine primi agentis, indeficienter agit; deficit autem in agendo, si contingat ipsum ab ordine primi agentis deflecti, sicut patet in instrumento, quum deficit a motu agentis. Dictum est autem quod, in ordine actionum moralium, duo principia voluntatem praecedunt, scilicet vis apprehensiva et objectum apprehensum, quod est finis. Quum autem unicuique mobili respondeat proprium motivum, non quaelibet vis apprehensiva est debitum motivum cujuslibet appetitus, sed hujus haec et illius alia. Sicut igitur appetitus sensitivi proprium motivum est vis apprehensiva sensualis, ita voluntatis proprium motivum est ratio ipsa.

"Rursus, quum ratio multa bona et multos fines apprehendere possit, cujuslibet autem sit proprius finis, et voluntatis erit objectum et finis et primum motivum, non bonum quodlibet, sed bonum quoddam determinatum. Quum igitur voluntas tendit in actum, mota ab apprehensione rationis repraesentantis sibi proprium bonum, sequitur debita actio. Quum autem voluntas in actione prorumpit ad apprehensionem apprehensivae sensualis vel ipsius rationis aliquod aliud bonum repraesentantis a proprio bono diversum, sequitur in actione voluntatis peccatum morale. Praecedit igitur in voluntate peccatum actionis defectus ordinis ad rationem et ad proprium finem. Ad rationem quidem, sicut quum, ad subitam apprehensionem sensus, voluntas in bonum delectabile secundum sensum tendit;

ad finem vero debitum, sicut quum ratio in aliquod bonum ratiocinando devenit quod non est vel nunc vel hoc modo bonum, et tamen voluntas in illud tendit quasi in proprium bonum. Hic autem ordinis defectus voluntarius est; nam in potestate ipsius voluntatis est velle et non velle; itemque est in potestate ipsius quod ratio actu consideret vel a consideratione desistat aut quod hoc vel illud consideret. Nec tamen iste defectus est malum morale; si enim ratio nihil consideret vel consideret bonum quodcumque, nondum est peccatum quousque voluntas in finem indebitum tendat; quod jam est voluntatis actus."

9.   Here it might be of use to meditate upon what St. Thomas teaches about the sin of omission (*Summa Theologica* I-II, q. 6, a. 3). Hs asks: Can we be guilty because our will did not act; can the will be engaged without acting, *utrum voluntarium possit esse sine actu?* And he answers, yes. "Illud cujus domini sumus, dicitur esse voluntarium. Sed nos domini sumus ejus quod est agere et non agere, velle et non velle. Ergo sicut agere et velle est voluntarium; ita et non agere et non velle."

The body of the article is as follows: "Dicendum quod voluntarium dicitur quod est a voluntate. Ab aliquo autem dicitur esse aliquid dupliciter. Uno modo, directe; quod scilicet procedit ab aliquo, inquantum est agens; sicut calefactio a calore. Alio modo, indirecte, ex hoc ipso quod non agit; sicut submersio navis dicitur esse a

gubernatore, inquantum desistit a gubernando. Sed
sciendum quod non semper id quod sequitur ad
defectum actionis, reducitur sicut in causam in
agens, ex eo quod non agit; sed solum tunc cum
potest et debet agere. Si enim gubernator non
posset navem dirigere, vel non esset ei commissa
gubernatio navis: non imputaretur ei navis submersio, quae per absentiam gubernatoris contin-
geret.

"Quia igitur voluntas, volendo et agendo, potest
impedire hoc quod est non velle et non agere, et
aliquando debet: hoc quod est non velle et non
agere imputatur ei, quasi ab ipsa existens. Et sic
voluntarium potest esse absque actu: quandoque
quidem, absque actu exteriori, cum actu interiori,
sicut cum vult non agere; *aliquando autem, et
absque actu interiori, sicut cum non vult agere.*"
In such a case that which causes the will to be
involved is not an act of not willing, but a non-
act of willing.

The answer to the third objection brings us
back to the theory of the voluntary non-consideration: "Dicendum quod eo modo requiritur ad
voluntarium actus cognitionis, sicut et actus voluntatis: ut scilicet sit in potestate alicuius considerare,
et velle, et agere. Et tunc sicut non velle et non
agere, cum tempus fuerit, est voluntarium; ita
etiam non considerare."

Now it must be carefully pointed out that in this
article, what St. Thomas has in view is the *sin of
omission.* The will can be condemned without
having acted and for not having acted; the will

may sin without acting, if it does not act at the
moment when it can and should act. Yet the free
and voluntary non-consideration of the rule, this
very non-act of consideration, is not in itself a sin
of omission; it does not constitute a sin, as long
as the very acting of the will is not produced with
the wound of that non-consideration, or (in the
case of the sin of omission) as long as the very
non-acting of the will does not take place instead
of the due acting, by virtue of that non-consideration. *Then* the free and voluntary non-consideration of the rule becomes a sin of omission, involved in every other sin of *commission* or *omission*. What I wished to stress in the article here
quoted, is that, either in the case of the sin of
omission or in the case of the free non-consideration of the rule, which precedes the sin, and
is not a sin in itself, *non-acting* may be free and
voluntary; in other words, there may exist a free
"initiative" *not to act*.

10. *De Veritate*, q. 5, a. 2.

11. *Summa Theologica* I-II, q. 112, a. 3, ad 2.—It
     might be said that when he avoids the divine mo-
     tion towards good, man is *no freer* than when he
     accepts this motion and acts for the good, but he
     is *more alone*. Truly he is then alone. Because in
     the case of good there are always two,—God and
     man; but in the case of evil (of evil as such,
     of the very privation which wounds the act)
     there is only one—man. In this case not only

is man free, but he has the *first*—negative and deficient—initiative. *Vae soli.* Man can be alone only in evil. (And definitely, it is this solitude that the damned prefer. They covet it and take pride in it, they have it, they can have it.)

The Aquinas Lectures

Published by the Marquette University Press,
Milwaukee 3, Wisconsin

The Nature and Origins of Scientism (1944) by John Wellmuth.

Cicero in the Courtroom of St. Thomas Aquinas (1945) by the late E. K. Rand, Ph.D., Litt.D., LL.D., Pope professor of Latin, *emeritus*, Harvard University.

St. Thomas and Epistemology (1946) by Fr. Louis-Marie Regis, O.P., Th.L., Ph.D., director of the Albert the Great Institute of Mediaeval Studies, University of Montreal.

St. Thomas and the Greek Moralists (1947, Spring) by Vernon J. Bourke, Ph.D., professor of philosophy, St. Louis University, St. Louis, Missouri.

History of Philosophy and Philosophical Education (1947, Fall) by Étienne Gilson of the *Académie française*, director of studies and professor of the history of mediaeval philosophy, Pontifical Institute of Mediaeval Studies, Toronto.

The Natural Desire for God (1948) by Fr. William R. O'Connor, S.T.L., Ph.D., former professor of dogmatic theology, St. Joseph's Seminary, Dunwoodie, N.Y.

St. Thomas and the World State (1949) by Robert M. Hutchins, former Chancellor of the University of Chicago.

Method in Metaphysics (1950) by Fr. Robert J. Henle, S.J., dean of the graduate school, St. Louis University, St. Louis, Missouri.

Wisdom and Love in St. Thomas Aquinas (1951) by Étienne Gilson of the *Académie française,* director of studies and professor of the history of mediaeval philosophy, Pontifical Institute of Mediaeval Studies, Toronto.

The Good in Existential Metaphysics (1952) by Elizabeth G. Salmon, associate professor of philosophy in the graduate school, Fordham University.

St. Thomas and the Object of Geometry (1953) by Vincent Edward Smith, Ph.D., professor of philosophy, University of Notre Dame.

Realism and Nominalism Revisited (1954) by Henry Veatch, Ph.D., professor of philosophy, Indiana University.

Imprudence in St. Thomas Aquinas (1955) by Charles J. O'Neil, Ph.D., professor of philosophy, Marquette University.

The Truth That Frees (1956) by Fr. Gerard Smith, S.J., Ph.D., professor and director of the department of philosophy, Marquette University.

St. Thomas and the Future of Metaphysics (1957) by Fr. Joseph Owens, C.Ss.R., associate professor of philosophy, Pontifical Institute of Mediaeval Studies, Toronto.

Thomas and the Physics of 1958: A Confrontation (1958) by Henry Margenau, Ph.D., Eugene Higgins professor of physics and natural philosophy, Yale University.

Uniform format, cover and binding.